The Advent Enrique in Panama

(In English)

Nayka Barrios Jaén

Illustrated by:

Sarah Fullerton-Barrios, Florida State University

Keke Cartoon - José García, Panama

Juan Sánchez, Panama

Digital Graphic Designer - Mayvi Espinosa, Panama

Dedication

I proudly dedicate this book to Panama, my beloved homeland.

To my mother Dilsa and my grandmother Frede

To all the "Enriques" in my family, including my father

To my grandmother "Flor" and aunt "Lily"

To my stepfather and friend "Beto"

To my uncle "Danilo" and the rest of the family who inspired the names and characters in this story.

Table of Contents

Acknowledgments

First and foremost, thank you to My Generation of Polyglots writers' group.

My class of 2025 at Shorecrest Preparatory School for your enthusiasm this year, for reading with me, and for giving your constructive comments. We had fun!

To my friends and beta readers, thank you for your support, constructive criticism, and encouragement throughout the development of this book:

- To my brother, Panamanian professor of folklore, Carlos Enrique Barrios Jaén, for sharing his practical advice.

- To Belén Johnson from Shorecrest Preparatory School, a national of Andalusia, for sharing her local knowledge.

- To my fairy godmothers and dear friends from Polk State College: Thelma Chicas, Rosalinda Collins, Lisa Gibilisco Rosa, and Arlene Torres.

- To my husband Peter for patiently listening and for brainstorming ideas in this writing adventure.

- To our family friend and world traveler John Kayser.

- To published author and friend Jerry McAbee for giving me his sage editorial advice.

These are the most frequently used words in the story.

Let's make predictions!

Preamble

At the end of class, the teacher distributes the **flyer**[1] to all students and says:

—"Here is more information for an adventure next summer."

Enrique is quick to respond.

—"Great! I'm going to talk to my family about the Exchange Program!"

---

1 flyer - volante

1 — Enrique

At Enrique's house, everyone gets up early for work and school.

—"Enrique, it's time to go to school," says his mother.

—**"I'm ready!**[1]**"** Enrique replies, and they leave for school.

Enrique is a 17-year-old boy, handsome, intelligent, and athletic. He loves soccer and outdoor activities. He likes science and mathematics, so he wants to go to college to study engineering. Enrique

likes his school very much; it is an International School.

His first class of the day is Spanish and Latin American history. The teacher, who is a native of Panama, is one of his favorite teachers.

—"Today we are going to start a new lesson," says the teacher while walking to the map. It will be a lesson on tales and legends of the Indigenous people of a region of Panama, and we will also learn how they maintain their traditions in today's world.

---

1 I am ready! - ¡Estoy listo!

—**"How Cool!"**[2] Enrique says. He and the rest of the class remain attentive. The teacher notices the interest and continues talking.

—"Let's start with Panama, my home country," says the teacher. "Where on August 15, 1519, Spain established the first Spanish city called Panama City in the Americas. This city still exists today and is the oldest city on the **Mainland**[3]. The first explorers called it Panama, "The Door of the Seas and the Key to the Universe.""

—"Wow!" another student says— "that's the place where the Panama Canal is, isn't it?"

—"Yes, that's right!" says the teacher with a smile. "Panama is a **narrow piece of land**[4], known as an isthmus that connects North and South America and has coasts on two oceans, the Atlantic and the Pacific. You can travel through, or alongside, the Panama Canal by boat, car or train; the distance is 50 miles (80.47 kilometers)..."

—"What a great idea!" says Enrique. "To go in less than an hour from one ocean to the other, that´s cool!"

—The teacher continues, "My country is small **but**[5] very beautiful, with **a lot of**[6] history, and you can do numerous outdoor activities. Class! To top it off, there are very interesting mountains, especially a mountain near a valley with a very old legend. That mountain is called *"La India Dormida"* some people say it is **enchanted**[7] by a beautiful Indigenous princess."

This information excites the class, especially the boys.

---

2 How cool! - ¡Qué guay!
3 Mainland - Tierra firme
4 narrow piece of land - istmo estrecho
5 but - pero
6 a lot of – mucho(a)/s
7 enchanted - encantada

—"Interesting!" says another boy.

The bell rings and the class finishes. The teacher **reminds**[8] them:

—"Boys and girls! Talk to your parents about Panama and the flyer about this summer's Exchange Program between Spain and Panama. If they accept, then you can go to Panama."

Enrique approaches the teacher, interested in the lesson, and says:

—"My family is part of Panama's history and I would really like to visit."

She appreciates the comment and with a smile reminds him to talk to his parents about the Exchange Program flyer.

---

8 reminds – ella les recuerda

2 — Nice People!

Enrique´s immediate family is small, just three people, Enrique and his parents. Enrique's parents are Spanish; the members of his family are descendants of a **landowner**[1] who received his land and his noble title of **Duke**[2], for working as an explorer for the Catholic King and Queen of Spain, Fernando and Isabel, around the year 1492.

Enrique and his parents have their **own business**[3]. It is a **farm of sunflowers**[4]. These yellow flowers are pretty, easy to cultivate, and very popular, because during the day **they turn**[5] to look for sunlight. In the countryside they cut the flowers and sell them. They **also**[6] sell the flowers' **seeds**[7] and the **oil**[8]. Tourists especially like to see these beautiful flowers.

---

1 landowners - terratenientes
2 duke - duque
3 own business - negocio propio
4 farm of sunflowers – granja de girasoles
5 they turn - giran
6 also - también
7 seeds - semillas
8 oil - aceite

During the week Enrique goes to school and on weekends he helps his parents in the sunflower business. Now it is Saturday morning, and Enrique talks to his father.

—"Father, are you going to need help in the sunflower field or the store today?" Enrique asks.

—"Yes, your mother is going to need help in the store, it's going to be a busy morning with the tourists."

In the afternoon, Enrique finishes helping his mother at the store and later goes to play a game of soccer with his friends. He has several friends and among them a best friend or BFF (*Best Friends Forever*), his name is Edilberto Barahona. Edilberto thinks his name is too long, so his parents and friends call him by his **nickname**[9] Beto. He is also Spanish, and they have both attended the same school since first grade.

Enrique and Beto love to eat **snacks**[10] and play video games after their soccer games. The boys also talk about the possibility of traveling to Panama and having their first adventure **without**[11] large school groups, their parents or chaperones.

Enrique says to Beto "I talked to my parents about the cultural exchange."

—"Tell me, what they said?" Beto asks.

—"They said yes... I can go!" Enrique says.

—"That is great!" says Beto. "My parents said yes, too."

—"Great! We're going to Panama!" They both shout for joy, "¡Olé, olé, olé, olé! ¡Panamá, Panamá!"

—"We have the best parents in the world!" says Enrique.

---

9 nickname - apodo
10 snack - merienda
11 without - sin

It's obvious that Enrique and Beto's parents **support**[12] him. They love that Enrique and Beto are friends. Their mothers are good friends too. They are going to coordinate the details of the cultural exchange trip between Spain and Panama that the boys want to experience.

---

12 support – ellos apoyan

3 — The exchange almost[1] begins!

There are only four days left of classes, Enrique and Beto are **very excited**[2] because they are going to Panama on August 1st. One of their classes is Design Entrepreneurship and Innovation (DEI). In this class the students learn how to organize the end of the year projects called **"Capstone projects"**[3].

These are very important projects because they are used to help improve or create solutions to a problem in society. At the end of 12th grade, the kids have to complete their projects. They are enthusiastic, **but**[4] they know that they need to work hard to prepare their projects.

But Enrique and Beto don't want to talk about school projects. For now, they just want to talk about their exchange trip

---

1 casi - almost
2 very excited – muy emocionados
3 Capstone project - proyecto final
4 but - pero

to Panama. The boys have already contacted the families that will host them in Panama to ask about the weather because they need to know what type of clothes they should pack in their suitcases.

—"We should wear comfortable clothes because Panama has tropical weather. It is very hot and very humid!" Enrique says.

—"He explains that Panama has two climatic seasons during the year; the **rainy season**[5] goes from April to November, and the **dry season**[6] goes from December to March." Beto reads this information from a Google search on his cellular phone.

They talk more and Beto says, "I'm a little nervous about our trip, I have never traveled by airplane, I always travel by train in **RENFE**[7]!"

—"Do not worry about it! It's okay! Beto. It's a long trip, and you can get plenty of sleep. You can also bring your phone and play video games," Enrique responds.

—"Enrique, are we going to have signal and mobile data on our phones during the flight?" asks Beto.

—"Yes, we are going to have signal and mobile data on our new smartphones, because my mother says she talked to your mother, and they are going to give us two mobiles with international connection," Enrique assures.

—"Perfect! Then we will have internet connection on our trip and in Panama. Super! Our mothers are so smart, they think of everything!" Beto comments.

—"**Of course!**[8] This way, we will communicate daily when we are separated in Panama."

---

5 rainy season - estación lluviosa
6 dry season - estación seca
7 RENFE - La Red Nacional de Ferrocarriles Españoles (RENFE) is the train system that connects Spain's main cities with Madrid, and it has Alta Velocidad (AVE) high speed trains.
8 Of course! - ¡Por supuesto!

4 — The Arrival

It is the first of August, and it is the rainy season in Panama. The airplane, in **which**[1] Enrique and Beto travel, arrives at Panama City's Tocumen International Airport. This is a very busy airport that connects many **flights**[2] from a lot of countries around the world with more than one hundred flights a day. It is summer in the north of the American continent and in Europe. It is also high season for tourism, so many people have time off and visit Panama.

The boys get out of the airplane, walk and talk:

—"Enrique, this airport is huge" Beto says, a little **overwhelmed**[3] by the noise. And at that moment, Beto sees his **host family**[4]. It's a couple with a little boy with a **paper sign**[5] that says "Beto". Beto sees the sign and approaches his host

---

1 Which - el cual
2 flights - vuelos
3 overwhelmed - abrumado
4 host family – familia anfitriona
5 paper sign - cartel

family. He greets them as they usually do in Spain, with a kiss on each cheek and hugs them; he is very happy to meet them in person. Beto says goodbye to Enrique.

—"Goodbye! Talk to you soon on the cellphone." Then he walks with his host family to the parking lot, and they leave in a car.

Instead, Enrique looks through the **crowd**[6] and does not see a sign with his name on it, nor his host family either. He is a little worried and confused. A few minutes later, he looks towards the airport gate and sees a very pretty girl looking at him in the crowd. She has a paper sign that says "Enrique." The girl looks very pretty and she appears to be about his age. He is **relieved**[7] and his **heart beats**[8] very fast as he walks up and talks to her.

They talk and introduce themselves, "Good afternoon, my name is Lily, and I am the daughter of your host family."

— Enrique is very happy and says, "Hi Lily, thank you for coming!"

—"I'm going to take you to our house. My mom doesn't drive her car in the city because she is **afraid**[9] to drive in Panama's traffic. There are too many cars in this crazy little city!" Lily explains.

—"**Oh my goodness!**[10] Well, Lily, you came for me at a good time. You are right, in the Internet search I saw that there is a lot of traffic and also that it is hot and humid in Panama!"

6 crowd – muchedumbre, muchas personas
7 relieved - aliviado
8 heart beats – corazón palpita
9 afraid - miedo
10 Oh my goodness! – ¡Santo cielo!

—"Enrique, you look very tired," says Lily. "Let's get on our way, so you can meet my parents in person. My mom and dad, Rosa and Danilo, are very nice and **hospitable**[11]."

---

11 hospitable - hospitalarios

5 — The Lucky Penny in the Parking Lot

In the airport parking lot Enrique walks with Lily to the car. Lily's car has a sticker with the **Uber**[1] logo on it. Enrique is confused because he has never taken an *Uber* **before**[2].

Suddenly[3], he sees a very shiny copper coin in the parking lot. Enrique learned in his English class about the *lucky penny*. He knows that if he sees a penny on the ground, he should pick it up and put it in his pocket to attract good luck. When he touches it, he feels an **unusual**[4] energy going through his body, but he thinks **he is just tired**[5] from the trip, so he puts the penny in his pocket.

Enrique and Lily leave the airport; she drives the car. There is a lot of traffic in Panama, but Lily looks very calm as she drives. She is a very nice girl. He wants to talk to her, but doesn't know what to say. He **takes out**[6] the penny of his pocket, looks at it, and thinks it is very shiny. Enrique talks to Lily about the penny.

—"Tell me, Lily, whose face is on the coin? It's different from the face on the Spanish penny."

---

1 Uber - Uber is a transportation company with an app that allows passengers to have a ride for a fee.
2 before - antes
3 suddenly - de repente
4 unusual - inusual
5 he is just tired – él solo está cansado
6 takes out - saca

14

—"In Panama, the pennies are made of **copper**[7]. The face on the penny is of the *Indio Urracá* who was an Indigenous leader who resisted Spanish colonization," Lily responds.

—"Oh, very interesting!" Enrique says. That conversation **reminds him**[8] that he needs to change euros to local money and he says "Lily, let's go to the bank please, I need to exchange euros for Panamanian currency."

—"No problem!" Lily responds and adds, "You know that here in Panama you can use the **balboa**[9] or the dollar. A balboa is worth the same as a dollar because we have an international banking system."

She smiles and continues driving. On the way Enrique sees many small stores with local products. He also sees lots of construction, because the Government of Panama is building a metro system.

---

7 copper - cobre, elemento químico
8 reminds him – le recuerda
9 Panama's official currency - el balboa

6 — Panama City

Enrique and Lily continue their tour, and he observes everything with great attention. They go along the *Corredor Sur*, which is a **highway**[1] that goes over the water in the Bay of Panama. Enrique can see *Panama La Vieja* and modern Panama City.

Then they enter Panama City through the ***Cinta Costera***[2] and drive-by *Avenida Balboa*. In the city, there are many **skyscrapers**[3] and Enrique sees a very large statue and asks, "Tell me Lily, who is the person on the monument?"

—Lily responds, "That is the statue of Vasco Núñez de Balboa. He was one of the Spanish explorers of the 1500s and

---

1 highway - autopista
2 Cinta Costera - Coastal Beltway
3 skyscrapers - rascacielos

that's why our currency is called the Balboa. He was the first Spaniard to see the Pacific Ocean from here."

—"Wow, what an interesting story!" Enrique says.

In a few minutes, Enrique admires the beautiful *Cerro Ancón* hill where a giant flag of Panama flies. On the slopes of the hill is Casco Viejo. It is the old original Colonial city and the Pacific entrance to the Panama Canal. Lily is still driving her *Uber*, and they enter a very large bridge, she points with her hand.

—"Enrique, we are now on the *Puente de las America's* over the Panama Canal. This bridge connects North America with South America. The Panama Canal is a very important waterway that connects the Pacific Ocean with the Atlantic Ocean. The Canal is very important for the world economy because of its strategic location."

Enrique is surprised and tries to take pictures of everything around him with his smartphone, —"**I don't want to forget**[4] any of this, Lily. I really like Panama, and I have been here for only two hours," Enrique smiles. "I'm so excited!"

They continue talking, he asks about the city, and they also talk about their schools. Lily says that she will graduate from high school this year too.

Enrique is impressed that Lily is so young to drive an *Uber* and asks:

4 I don´t want to forget – No quiero olvidar

—"Hey Lily, you are very young. At your age, are you allowed to drive an *Uber* car?"

—"Yes, here in Panama, I can drive with a special permit during the day until 9:00 p.m.," Lily says. "I drive to take visitors from the airport to *El Valle*."

—"Lily, you are really brave to drive in this traffic!" — Enrique says with a **chuckle**[5].

—"No, I'm not brave at all, my friends think I'm a little crazy, ha ha! What I like the most is that when I drive I get to meet a lot of people and I also earn some money for college. This is just temporary."

Enrique talks more about his life in Spain, his friend Beto and also that they will graduate from high school this year. They

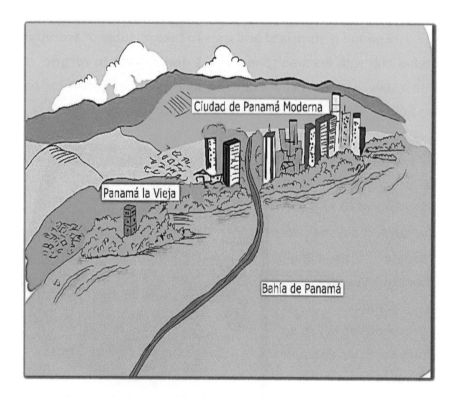

---

5 chuckle – risa baja y entre dientes

talk some more while she makes a quick stop at the bank for Enrique to change his money.

They are already close to the family's house. Enrique is excited and curious because he wants to know more about the place where he will be living for the next few weeks.

—"Lily, **I am eager**[6] to learn more about this country, its culture, and you, my host family!"

Finally[7], after almost one hour, they arrive at a small hotel in a valley. Enrique **is a little surprised**[8] and does not understand.... Why doesn't Lily take him to a house? Why are they stopping in a place that doesn't look like a normal house?

---

6 I am eager - tengo muchas ganas
7 Finally - finalmente
8 is a little surprised – está un poco sorprendido

7 — An Inn

Lily and her family live in a house that is also **an inn**[1]. They are the **owners**[2] of the inn, because it is a family business. Enrique just found out that he is going to live in an inn, which is very interesting for him. The parents are Mr. Danilo and Mrs. Rosa. The hostess and boss of the inn is Mrs. Rosa, that's why the inn is called La Posada de Rosa. The inn is located in *El Valle de Antón*. The inn is a hotel, but smaller. Travelers and tourists like to visit it because it is **cheaper than a**[3] hotel and provides a friendlier experience.

Mrs. Rosa is very happy to finally meet Enrique in person. Enrique thinks that Rosa and Lily are special names because they

---

1 an inn - un hostal
2 owners - dueños
3 cheaper than a – más barato que

are names of flowers. Mrs. Rosa **meets**[4] Enrique and is very happy.

—"Welcome Enrique! I'm Rosa, your host mother."

—"Hello! Thank you very much! Nice to meet you, Mrs. Rosa."

—"Just call me, Rosa, please!" She hugs him immediately and continues talking, "I hope that you enjoyed the *Uber* ride and the Panama traffic from the airport, ha ha!"

—"Yes! I enjoyed it very much, Rosa. Thank you!" Enrique says.

—"Enrique, this is my dad, Danilo Tapir," Lily says.

—"Nice to meet you, Mr. Danilo," Enrique says and **shakes his hand**[5].

—"Nice to meet you, young man. Please call me Danilo. Welcome to *El Valle!*"

—"Thank you very much, Danilo!"

—"**Don't mention it**[6], Enrique!"

—"I'm so happy to finally be here with you!"

Enrique wants to be nice, but he feels very tired from the trip. Mrs. Rosa gives him the key to the room where he is going to stay and also gives him the Wi-Fi password on a piece of paper. The key has a **key ring**[7] made of wood with the number eight on it. Enrique doesn't think much about it, but he does think it's a coincidence that the room is number eight, like his birthday, and his lucky number.

In his room, Enrique sees a tourist brochure with a QR code to listen to a podcast. He uses his smartphone with an international

---

4 s/he meets – él/ella conoce
5 shake hands - le da la mano
6 don't mention it - estamos a la orden
7 key ring - llavero

signal to scan the code. On the website, he can see information about the area where the inn is located and thinks it is a wonderful place. He listens to an audio about *El Valle de Antón*, but Enrique is very tired, so he falls asleep listening to the audio.

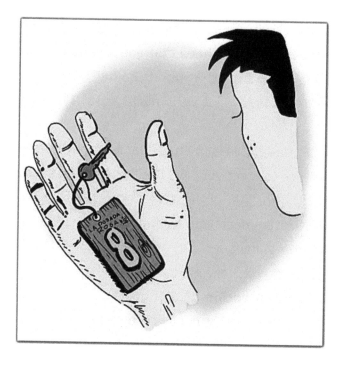

8 — The Panamanian Breakfast, Delicious!

It is Saturday morning. Enrique **wakes up**[1], takes a shower, and feels full of energy. He goes to the dining room to have breakfast. He has the opportunity to talk to Mrs. Rosa, Lily, Mr. Danilo, and other people who are at the inn.

—"Good morning, Rosa! How are you today?"

—"Good Enrique! I am doing well. Did you sleep well?"

—"Yes, I always sleep well when I'm very tired, ha ha!"

—"I imagine you did because your trip from Spain to Panama is very long. There are seven-hours of difference."

Mr. Danilo waves while he eats his ***carimañolas***[2] and drinks his black coffee.

—"Good morning, Enrique! Please sit down at our table."

Enrique sits down and begins to eat breakfast. He doesn't know what he's eating, but he thinks it's all very delicious and exclaims:

1wakes up – se despierta
2 carimañolas – frituras hechas de puré de yuca que se rellena con pollo, carne de res o queso antes de ser fritas

23

—"What is this I'm eating? It's very delicious. Is it an empanada or a stuffed potato?"

—"It's a *carimañola* made with yucca dough and stuffed with ground meat!" Mrs. Rosa smiles and explains, while Lily smiles.

—"Thank you for the explanation, yummy! They are delicious! I really like *carimañolas,*" Enrique says as he enjoys the new flavors and smiles.

Enrique eats five *carimañolas*, coffee, and fresh cheese. He is very hungry! He eats and continues talking to Mrs. Rosa and the people at the table.

—"Rosa, I learned about Panama and some legends in my Latin American history class. I also listened to a *podcast* about this valley. There is a legend about the mountain and the crater of a volcano that I want to know more about."

—"Oh, yes! Of course, Enrique," Mrs. Rosa says, there are several legends. Danilo knows the legends very well, and he is always ready to tell them. Danilo knows the history of the Indigenous tribes in Panama because he is a native of *El Valle* and his family is a descendant of an Indigenous chief.

—"Of course!" Mr. Danilo assures and begins to tell the legend of *Flor del Aire*. "This story was told to me by my **great-grandfather**[3] like this..."

---

3 great-grandfather - bisabuelo

9 — The Legend of *Cacique Urracá* and *Flor del Aire*

—"*Many years ago in a place in the 'New World' that is now Panama,*" Mr. Danilo says, "*There was an Indigenous tribe. This tribe still exists, they are very hard-working people with very beautiful and intelligent women. When the Spanish arrived, the Indigenous chief was* **Cacique**[1] *Urracá, the most courageous warrior who fought against the European explorers in the lands of Panama.*

The Cacique had a beautiful daughter" Mr. Danilo continues, "*Princess Flor del Aire, who was engaged to be married to Yaraví who was a young, strong Indigenous warrior. But sadly, the princess had no love for him, because she was in love with a Spaniard.*

Yaraví, realizing that Flor del Aire did not feel love for him, suffered greatly, and in his despair he **jumped**[2] *from the mountain, where he lost his life.* **After that**[3]*, Flor del Aire promised*

---

1 Cacique – indigenous chief
2 jumped - saltó
3 After that – Después de eso

to forget her Spanish love and started crying and **wandering**[4] around the forest for a long time. One day, Flor del Aire fell asleep crying on the top of the mountain on the green grass. Feeling sorry for her, the mountain covered her with a **blanket**[5] of vegetation, and as a result immortalized her. That is how her silhouette has remained visible as a great symbol of her love. Many people believe in the legend and say that Yaraví is the sleeping volcano. Experts also claim that the valley is the crater of a dormant volcano with small hills and rocks."

—"Wow! Danilo, that's an **amazing**[6] legend, but too romantic for me," Enrique says. "I don't like romanticism, I like hiking, ha ha! I want you to tell me more about the volcano, please. Where is it?"

Mr. Danilo is not very impressed with Enrique's reaction and does not smile.

—"No, Enrique, it is not 100% romantic. When you get a chance to walk the trails, immerse yourself in the springs, and climb the mountain, you will understand its meaning much better."

Enrique is a little **embarrassed**[7] with Mr. Danilo because he thinks he doesn't take the story seriously and he says:

—"I'm sorry, Danilo! I promise I will respect the history and legends of Panama because I want to learn more about this country, okay!"

—"To answer your last question," Mr. Danilo adds, "the volcano is **under**[8] our feet. *El Valle de Antón* is the crater of a dormant volcano."

---

4 wandering - vagando
5 blanket - manta
6 amazing - asombrosa
7 embarrassed - avergonzado
8 under – debajo

Enrique is amazed and **eagerly**[9] wants to know more about *El Valle de Antón* and its legends. Mr. Danilo gets up from the table and he says:

—"Well, another time we will talk more about this topic. It is already late and time to go to the market. We have to help prepare the open-air-market for tomorrow, Sunday." —Mr. Danilo adds, "Lily, remember that you have to go to the airport to pick up other tourists, please."

—"Yes, Dad," Lily says.

—"Enrique, if you want, you can come by the market later."

—"Okay Danilo!" Enrique says.

—"See you later!" Mr. Danilo responds as he says goodbye to everyone.

---

9 eagerly - con entusiasmo

10 — Enrique and Beto Communicate

Although Panama is a small country with a great variety of landscapes, such as the cordillera, which is a **paradise**[1] at more than 800 meters above **sea level**[2]. *El Valle* has a cool and pleasant climate. Panama also has beaches on two oceans.

The house of Beto's host family is on a beach called Costa Esmeralda. This beach is 30 minutes away from the inn where Enrique is staying.

As they promised to communicate with their cellular phones, Enrique writes a short text to Beto.

—"Hello Beto! Can you talk?"

—"Yes," Beto responds with a text and "ring ring!" his cellular phone rings immediately.

—"Hello, Beto! How are you?"

—"Hello, Enrique! I'm doing great, and you?"

—"I'm fine too," Enrique says. "**Though**[3] my host family is a little different because they don't live in a house. They live in an-inn."

---

1 paradise - paraíso
2 sea level - nivel del mar
3 though – aunque, sin embargo

—"Wow!" Beto says, "what a surprise, ha ha! My host family lives in a house on the beach on the Pacific Ocean side. The beach is called Costa Esmeralda."

—Enrique adds, "The strangest thing is that my family has an *Uber* driver who picked me up at the airport. Her name is Lily and she is the daughter of my host family. She is very smart and pretty. This place is called *El Valle de Antón*."

—"That´s so cool Enrique! Then we can take an *Uber* ride in Panama. Awesome! Today, Saturday I will be at the beach with my family, but I want to visit you in *El Valle* tomorrow, Sunday!" Beto says.

—"Great! The town has an open-air-market on Sundays. Many people visit this market to buy handicrafts and fresh products such as fruits and vegetables. I can ask Lily if she can drive her *Uber* to your house and bring you here. We can meet at the market here in *El Valle!*" Enrique says.

—"Good idea! You text me when Lily answers back. I will also share my GPS location," Beto says.

—"Yes, I will text Lily, and I will let you know her answer," Enrique says.

Enrique is very excited that he will probably see his friend Beto tomorrow. When he finishes his conversation with Beto, he texts Lily, and asks if she can pick up his friend Beto tomorrow.

— She texts back, "yes".

Immediately, Enrique texts Beto and confirms that Lily will pick him up in her Uber.

After that, Enrique goes to the Central Park market and helps Mr. Danilo and other **locals**[4] in *El Valle* to set up **tents**[5] for the Sunday market. Enrique works very late and falls asleep very tired.

El Pueblo de El Valle   El volcán dormido

---

4 locals - lugareños
5 tents - carpas

11 — The Boys Explore the Town

It is Sunday morning and Enrique wakes up, eats his breakfast, and talks to Mrs. Rosa and Mr. Danilo, and the people at the inn.

—"Where is Lily?" Enrique asks them.

—"She ate her breakfast early and left in her *Uber* to work and to pick up your friend Beto," Mr. Danilo answers.

—"Wow! She is a very good and punctual girl," Enrique says and smiles.

—"Yes, she is also a **hard-working**[1] girl," Mrs. Rosa says.

Enrique smiles and hopes with all his heart that he will be able to see Lily later. He also knows it is going to be a very good day because he is going to see his friend Beto. So he talks with other people at the inn about the weather and *El Valle*, and then he walks out to the local market.

As promised, Lily drops Beto in the Plaza and Lily goes to run errands with her mom. Enrique and Beto **get together**[2] in the

---

1 hard-working - trabajadora
2 get together - se reúnen

park at *Plaza del Parque Central*. They are very happy to see each other **again**[3]. They are curious to visit the market and learn more about the town of *El Valle*.

Enrique says:

—"Beto, you know this valley is also known as the place of the legend of the mountain of *La India Dormida*. Look at the mountain over there on the left, it is shaped like a woman who is asleep. The legend is very **sappy**[4], can you believe she died of love? Ha ha!"

—"Really Enrique? I think it's a very cool legend. We can visit the mountain, do you want to do some **hiking**[5]?"

—"Good idea, you know, some people also say that *El Valle* is a sleeping volcano. People believe the volcano is the brave Indigenous warrior who died for *La India Dormida*. There are also rumors that there are **goblins**[6] and ghosts on the trail."

Beto is curious to know more about the trail and asks Enrique, "How long do you think it will take us to climb the mountain?"

—"I don't know, but look there in the center of the park. There is a statue and a map. Let's go see!" Enrique answers.

In the center of the park, the boys look at the statue of the Indigenous princess *Flor del Aire*. The princess's face looks very familiar. It is almost the same as Lily's face, but they think it is a coincidence. They also look at and read the map of the town and *La India Dormida* Trail.

---

3 again – nuevamente, de nuevo
4 sappy - cursi
5 hiking - senderismo
6 goblins - duendes

Beto reads and tells Enrique, "Look here, it says *El Valle* has a museum and a small zoo. Popular activities are hiking the mountain trail, swimming in the natural hot and cold springs."

Enrique reads another section of the map and adds, "There are **square shaped trees**[7] and petroglyphs called *Piedra Pintada*. Also, *El Valle* is the home of the Panamanian **golden frogs**[8]."

The boys are excited about all the things they are going to learn about, and so they continue to walk around the market and learn about the local culture. They look for local food for lunch. They eat rice with chicken and drink **chicheme**[9].

While talking about what they are going to do the next day, they walk and arrive at a park where there are many people playing dominoes. They see Mr. Danilo playing with several other people at a table.

Mr. Danilo greets them from a distance and says, "Come in closer, boys."

---

7 square shaped trees - árboles cuadrados
8 golden frogs - ranas doradas
9 chicheme - una bebida que se encuentra casi exclusivamente en Panamá hecha al hervir maíz dulce con canela, vainilla, leche y azúcar al gusto.

12 —The Dominoes Game at Parque de los Aburridos

Mr. Danilo goes to a park every Sunday with his friends after helping the townspeople with things for the local market. The *Parque de Los* **Aburridos**[1] is a famous park in Panama, but the truth is that it is not boring at all...

—"Enrique, Beto! Do you know how to play dominoes?" Mr. Danilo asks. Enrique and Beto look at him, but they **didn´t say anything**[2]. —"If you don't know how, you can learn here!" Mr. Danilo says.

They smile and sit at a table, and play for two hours, having fun and talking to local people. They drink coconut water, which they love coconut water because it is cold and refreshing. Not only that, but they also eat *empanadas*[3], and green mango salad with vinegar, salt and pepper.

Suddenly, Enrique receives a text from Lily. Enrique feels very happy, and his face gets very red. He replies to her with a short text.

Beto asks, "What's wrong, Enrique? Who is texting you? You look silly, and your face is red as a tomato."

---

1 bored people - aburridos
2 didn´t say anything - nada
3 empanadas - empanadas son discos de masa rellenos y cocinados fritos u horneados.

—"It's all right, Beto! It's Lily who wants to talk, maybe she's coming to play dominoes with us."

Beto says, "I don't think so Enrique, you're crazy! Lily has to work on her *Uber.*"

A few seconds later, Lily calls "ring, ring!"

—"Hello!" Enrique answers his phone.

—"Hello, Enrique! It's Lily, I'm near *El Valle*. Tell me, does Beto need to go back to the beach with his host family? If so, I can give him a ride."

—"Thanks Lily, but Beto is going to stay in *El Valle* tonight because tomorrow we are going hiking. We are going to visit the waterfalls and the *La India Dormida* trail."

—"That's great! Well then, I will see you tonight at the inn for dinner," Lily says.

—"Sounds perfect Lily, see you later," Enrique says.

—"Okay, bye **guys**[4]!" Lily says.

---

4 guys – chicos/chicas o ambos

13 — Dinner and Conversation

El mejor estofado de Panamá

It is Sunday afternoon and time for dinner at *La Posada de Rosa*, and all the guests gather to eat. Today Mrs. Rosa cooks her famous **pork stew**[1], the house special with white rice, *plátanos maduros* and for dessert *Dulce Tres Leches*. The inn has a five-star rating on Google, which describes the stew as delicious.

Enrique and Beto arrive in the dining room and a little later Lily arrives and greets them. Beto greets Lily with two kisses on the cheeks and a hug, as it is done in Spain. Enrique on the other hand gets very nervous, his face turns red as a tomato again, and he doesn't know what to do, but Lily approaches him and greets him with a kiss on the cheek and a hug as it is done in Panama. It is very common in Latin America and Europe to greet with one or

---

1 pork stew - estofado de cerdo

two kisses and a hug when you see an acquaintance. Enrique's heart is beating very fast:

—"Hi Lily!! I'm so glad you're already here," Enrique says excitedly.

—"Hi guys! What's up?" Lily says as she smiles.

—"Beto and I are here waiting for...! Well, waiting for the food! We are very hungry," —Enrique says with a chuckle.

—"Good thing you're hungry! Because today there is a delicious pork-stew. I'm going to the kitchen to help my mom. She is very busy," Lily says as she walks towards the kitchen.

Half an hour later..., Enrique, Beto, Lily, Mrs. Rosa, and Mr. Danilo sit down to enjoy the food. They talk happily about everything they saw in *El Valle*, when they arrived at the park and when they played dominoes. Then Enrique says:

—"Tomorrow, Beto and I are going hiking in the mountains. Do you have any recommendation for us?"

Mr. Danilo gives them important information.

—"Walking along the trail takes about four hours, you can see the *Piedra Pintada* and several **waterfalls**[2]. The waterfalls are called: **Chorro**[3] *de Los Enamorados, Salto del Sapo, Chorro Escondido,* and *Chorro de La* **Moza**[4]."

—"You can swim and cool off in the water," Lily adds. There is a lot of green vegetation and a wonderful view at more than 800 meters above sea level. It is also cold at the top.

—"Oh! and you have to bring a snack and water," Mrs. Rosa recommends, "...and there are snakes, so you have to wear sneakers or hiking boots, not **flip-flops**[5] or *Crocs*."

---

2 waterfall - cascada
3 Chorro – torrente de agua
4 Moza - término formal y antiguo para una joven doncella
5 flip flops - chancletas/chanclas

—"**Sounds exciting**[6]! It's going to be a lot of fun, Lily, are you coming with us?" Beto asks and looks at Enrique as Enrique smiles and his cheeks turn red.

Lily declines the invitation and says, "I like the idea, but I cannot go, tomorrow is my day off, and I have to **run errands**[7] with my mom. But, I can go at the end of the day to see you at the exit of the trail."

Enrique replies, "Sorry you cannot come with us, but we will see you at the end of the trail. **Still**[8], it's going to be a great adventure for Beto and me."

Mr. Danilo gets up from the table and tells them:

—"Well guys, let's all go rest, tomorrow you have an adventurous day ahead of you, and you need all the energy to climb the mountain!"

—"Danilo is right, tomorrow you will need a lot of energy. Let's go to sleep!" Mrs. Rosa adds.

She goes to close the **gate**[9] of the inn's patio and exclaims:

—"Oh how nice! It's raining and it's fantastic! Because it means we're going to have a cool night to sleep without hot

---

6 Sounds exciting - suena emocionante
7 to run errands - hacer mandados
8 Still - Todavía
9 gate - portón

temperatures. Also, tomorrow is going to be a comfortable day for you."

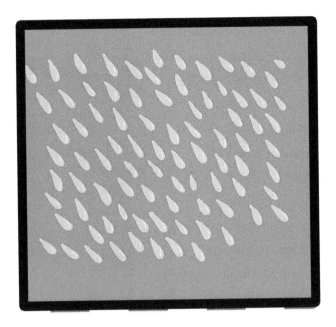

14 — Paper Map or GPS?

It's 6:00 a.m. in *El Valle de Antón* and nobody needs an alarm clock, because the roosters and hens get up when the sun rises and the roosters start crowing.

—"**¡Quiquiriquí! ¡Quiquiriquí!**[1]"

Enrique and Beto get up and get ready for their journey, they go to the dining room to have breakfast. Enrique drinks coffee with milk and Beto orange juice. They wear comfortable clothes sneakers, sunglasses, and hats. Also, they take water, cereal bars, and cellphones with GPS.

—"Good morning! Are you ready?" Lily asks them.

—"Ready!" answer Enrique and Beto. So Lily goes with them to the entrance of the mountain trail. At the entrance there are adults and children who are local guides for the visitors, they are wearing hats in the shapes of typical Panamanian animals such as: golden frogs, toucans, monkeys, **spiders**[2], horses, and tapirs. The man wearing the tapir hat looks familiar; in Panama, a tapir is a wild pig and is also known as a **macho de monte**[3]. Enrique approaches and sees that it is Mr. Danilo Tapir, now Enrique

---

1 ¡Quiquiriquí! ¡Quiquiriquí! - Onomatopeya o escritura en español para el sonido de un gallo. En inglés se escribe cock-a-doodle-do
2 spiders - arañas
3 tapir or wild pig - macho de monte

understands why Mr. Danilo knows the history of the mountain so well.

—"Hi guys, good morning and welcome to the trail of the India Dormida!" Mr. Danilo says.

—"What a surprise to see you here. Lily, why didn't you tell us that Danilo works here?" Enrique says with a surprised face.

—"Oh, it's just very normal, so **I** always **forget**[4] that detail," Lily answers.

—"No problem!" Enrique says.

Mr. Danilo offers them paper maps, but the boys don't take them, they think the GPS on their cellphones are enough.

At the entrance there is an Indigenous girl wearing a golden frog hat selling **handicrafts**[5] in the shape of small green and gold frogs made of ceramic. She also sells mangoes, coconut water, *platanitos*, coconut candies, and *pepitas de marañón*[6].

Tourists buy handicrafts as souvenirs, and snacks for the trail. Enrique and Beto buy coconut candies, *platanitos*, and cold

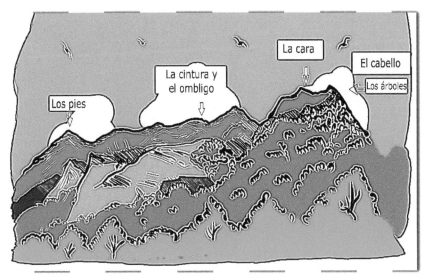

---

4 I forget - se me olvida
5 handicrafts - artesanías
6 cashew nuts - pepitas de marañón

coconut water in bottles for their snacks. Other children are also wearing hats in the shape of animals offering to be **tour guides**[7], but Enrique replies:

—"No, thanks, kids! You guys are very nice, but we don't need tour guides, we have our GPS on our phones. We want to go alone to have our own adventure, thank you!"

---

7 tourist guides - guías turísticos

15 — The Trail and the Volcano

Enrique and Beto enter the trail, walk for thirty minutes and see the *Piedra Pintada* hieroglyphics. Some people think that it is an Indigenous map of *El Valle*. Also, they see a lady coming down with her shoes in her hand, her purse in the other hand to go to work. They greet her and continue walking up the mountain.

They walk for another thirty minutes and are amazed. The weather is cool because they are already in the forest of tall trees. There are also wild orchid flowers of many colors everywhere. This is the head and the "hair of *La India*" …

—"Look Beto! There are toucans over there on the right. Take a picture," Enrique says.

In the middle of the trees, they see a big **sloth bear**[1] moving very, very slowly.

—"Take more pictures, Beto! This is sensational!" Enrique says.

---

1 sloth bear - oso perezoso

—"But Enrique, you have to take pictures with your cellphone too, because my battery only has three bars, okay?"

—"Okay Beto!" Enrique says.

So under a very hot sun and cool wind, they follow the road and after 30 minutes more they arrive at the *Chorro de Los Enamorados*. The two boys are amazed.

Enrique shouts with excitement, "Beto, let's go for a swim! Quick, let's go into the waterfall. It looks cool!"

Enrique wants to swim, also he wants to take a selfie in that beautiful place. He takes his cellular phone out of his pocket, and it falls-out of his **sweaty hands**[2]. Enrique **quickly**[3] jumps into the water.

—"Oh no, no, no, no! My cellphone! It's soaked!!!"

—"Phew! How lucky" Beto assures, our cellphones are waterproof, as always our mothers think of everything. If the phones get **soaked**[4] they won't get damaged, ha ha!

—"Yes, **that's lucky!**"[5] Enrique says. **I hope**[6] it works well the rest of the way because we didn't take the paper map Danilo offered us.

---

2 sweaty hands - manos sudorosas
3 quickly - rápidamente
4 they soaked - se mojan
5 that's lucky! - ¡qué suerte!
6 I hope - Ojalá

They use Beto's cellular phone to take pictures and continue their adventure.

—"Yay!" Beto says and jumps into the water from the highest rock.

They swim for 15 minutes, get out of the water and dry off, and eat their snacks. They put into practice what they know about taking care of nature and put the garbage in their backpacks so as not to damage the trail's ecosystem. Then they get ready to continue walking.

They walk ten minutes more, go very carefully up another very **steep hill**[7] and arrive at the "**throat**"[8] of *La India*. From there, they enjoy the beautiful view of the crater of the sleeping volcano that forms *El Valle*.

They continue until they reach the **stone steps**[9] that are very high because they go up to the "**chest**"[10] of *La India*. When they reach the top, they can see some beautiful plants and aerial flowers like orchids, Panama´s national flower.

Suddenly, Enrique feels a mild tremor, as if the volcano is waking-up under their feet. Also... they hear screams.

—"Hello, hello, hello! Oh, my God! Hello, hello, hello!"

—"Is it a woman?" Enrique wonders.

---

7 steep hill - cerro muy empinado
8 throat - garganta
9 stone steps - escalera de piedra
10 chest - pecho

16 — The Voices

Enrique looks at Beto, they hear voices and shouts again "Hello, hello, hello!"

They worry, walk for two more minutes and see no one. They are already on the path by the "**waist**"[1] and the "**navel**"[2] of *La India* and then between the trees they see two big birds, two red, green, blue, and yellow **macaws**[3] that sing and talk.

—"Hello, hello, hello! Oh, my God! Ha ha ha!"

Enrique and Beto start laughing because the macaws **frightened them**[4] and are so funny.

—"Oh my goodness, I'm glad no one is in danger, and it's just those crazy birds, ha ha!" Beto says.

Enrique remembers that there are many myths about this mountain, plus there are **ghosts**[5] and elves. Enrique is a little scared, but continues walking and comments:

---

1 waist - cintura
2 belly button - ombligo
3 macaws - guacamayas
4 frightened them - los asustaron
5 ghost - fantasma

—"In the podcast I listened to, they mention the ghost of *Flor del Aire*."

—"How scary, Enrique! Shut up and don't say **silly things**[6]. We have to walk fast to get to the end of the trail, besides, it's very hot. I hope it rains!"

They continue walking and now the weather is a little windy. They see some boys **flying kites**[7]. Enrique and Beto say hello and stop to take pictures of the valley. They are already close to the *Chorro de La Moza*.

—"We have to hurry to *Chorro de La Moza* to take another quick dip in the water and take a **nap**[8]. Let's go fast, Enrique!"

As if by magic the weather gets cooler, there is a nice wind and the sun's rays **sparkle**[9] as a gift from Mother Nature. The boys reach the waterfall without any problems. Enrique and Beto are amazed:

—"Wow, Beto, this place is even more fascinating than

---

6 silly things - tonterías
7 flying kites - están volando cometas
8 nap - siesta
9 sparkle - brillan

the previous spring! It's a good place to make our *TikTok* #Panama"

—"Yes! Good idea, this is amazing. There is fresh water and thermal water coming out of the volcano. Let's go for a swim first, Yay! Wooohooo!!" Beto says.

This time, Enrique takes his cellular phone out of his pocket very carefully before entering the water to swim and looks at it, and sees a problem.

—"Oh, Beto, my cellphone isn´t working properly because it is wet after I drop it in the *Chorro de Los Enamorados*. My GPS isn´t working, either."

—"But Enrique, if our cellphones are waterproof, why isn't yours working?"

—"Yes, you're right, but the screen is broken, noooo!" Enrique exclaims.

—"Don't worry! Let me check my phone" Beto says. "Oh, oh! My battery is **almost dead**[10]. We have to take another selfie soon."

—"Okay, it's okay," Enrique says. "Don't worry, we have to enjoy this moment here."

Enrique and Beto sit on the **edge**[11] of the river talking quietly and want to take a nap; but again, they feel a mild tremor in the earth under their feet.

At first the air is calm, and then as if by magic, there is a fresh wind again. The boys notice the fragrance of flowers and watch the waters move. At the same time, they hear a very sweet voice speaking to them. They can see a beautiful woman in the water combing her shiny black hair, but in reality it is a ghost that

_____

10 almost dead (battery) - casi muerta
11 edge – orilla (del río)

looks very much like Lily. They cannot believe what they see, and Enrique says:

—"How strange! It cannot be Lily, she's with Mrs. Rosa..."

—"You're right..." Beto says in a frightened voice.

17 — The Ghost in the Spring

Enrique and Beto do not understand what is happening, because what they see is very beautiful and does not seem real. They are confused, but **enchanted**[1].

—"Hello!" She swims, and smiles as she speaks to them, "Thank you for coming to visit our trail and the mountain!"

—"Lily, is that you?" Beto asks.

—"No, I am not Lily. I am *Flor del Aire, La India Dormida*."

Enrique and Beto look at **each other**[2] in amazement without being able to speak, Enrique finds the courage to say:

—"*Flor del Aire*, are you *La India Dormida* of the Mountain? But you look like Lily."

1 enchanted - encantados
2 each other – el uno al otro

Flor del Aire explains, "Yes, Lily, her father Danilo and I have the same native origin, that's why we **look alike**[3]. They also belong to the *Sociedad Secreta de La India Dormida* (SSID) and their mission is to attract visitors to the trail. Yaraví, my eternal lover, is now the sleeping volcano that causes the gentle tremors. It is very important that a volcano stays calm to **avoid**[4] the eruption of hot lava, for this reason it is very good for us when people who respect and appreciate our culture and history visit us."

—"Wow!" Enrique says.

—"¡Double wow!" Beto says.

Flor del Aire continues, "We need more people to visit the trail so that the Yaraví volcano does not feel so lonely, as visitors keep it happy and peaceful. SSID has the goal of taking care of the mountain to avoid **hate**[5] and harm. The Volcano on the other hand continues to admire my precious mountain, India Dormida."

—"That's all very important!" Enrique says.

—"Yes!" Beto assures.

—*Flor Del Aire* comments further, "Because of my loyalty to our tribe, the Gods allow me to come down from the mountain to this spring to talk to the travelers and dream that someday I will see my love Carlos Dominguez. He was a Spanish explorer."

—Enrique says, "Dominguez? How fascinating, that's my last name, and I'm from Spain. My ancestor who came to America in the 1500s was named Carlos Dominguez."

Flor del Aire says "Enrique, you are a descendant of Carlos! That's why destiny brought you to Panama, what joy I feel in my heart!!"

---

3 look alike - parecerse
4 avoid - evitar
5 hate - odio

Enrique thinks about all the things that happened to him since his arrival in Panama, and now he understands better... he remembers the lucky penny in the parking lot and the energy he felt when he touched it... he also remembers the number eight as his birthday and what he felt when his teacher told them about the exchange trip to Panama. It all makes sense now!

Beto on the other hand feels frightened and opens his big eyes and asks, "Miss *Flor del Aire*, what do you want from us? How can we help you?"

Flor del Aire answers, "**you have helped a lot**[6] by respecting our culture and taking care of nature, by not littering our village, *El Valle* and the trail. The spirits of our ancestors are very appreciative of your actions to maintain peace between the races."

Suddenly, the scent of flowers is stronger, and *Flor del Aire* disappears as if by magic. Enrique and Beto look at each other like crazy, unable to believe what they saw. They cannot believe it and think, did they really see *Flor del Aire* or was it all part of a vision?

It gets dark, and their cellular phone batteries are almost dead. They cannot believe what happened. They take their things, put on their sneakers and walk very quickly.

—"I hope we are not lost, next time we need to bring a paper map," Beto comments.

They reach the end of the trail and suddenly see Lily in the distance. They look at each other and wonder, is it Lily or is it *La India Dormida* again?

—"Lily! Lily! It's you, we're so happy to see you," Enrique says. You're going to think we're crazy, but we saw a vision.

—"What are you guys talking about?" Lily smiles.

---

6 you have helped a lot - han ayudado mucho

—"At first we thought it was you," Beto says.

—"Oh no! Sorry guys," Lily **laughs**[7].

—"Don't laugh Lily, at first we felt a little panic, we thought it was you, and then we thought it was a ghost...but then we knew it was a vision of *La India Dormida*," Enrique says.

—"Ufff! Don't panic guys. *Flor del Aire* is the cheerful spirit and the guardian of the mountain who is very respectful and proud of her tribe. Many local people are secret members of the SSID. I am one of them myself, we help take care of the mountain. We need more people who want to be part of the society, because we are working to reforest the mountain. If you come up with a good idea, you are welcome to be part of the society."

—"This is all very interesting. I'm interested in helping SSID, I will think about it," Enrique replies. "My family in Spain has a sunflower farm."

—"This is all very exciting, but it's darkening. After this adventure, I'm very tired and very hungry. Shall we continue talking on the way home?" Beto asks.

Enrique and Beto return with Lily to the inn. They have dinner together and talk about their experiences on the trail and the mountain. When they

---

7 laughs - ríe

finish dinner, the boys and Lily dance like macaws for a *TikTok* #Panama challenge.

After that, Lily takes Beto in her *Uber* back to his host family's house on the beach.

The rest of the week, the boys **spend more time**[8] with their host families and get to know the culture and traditions of Panama better.

Beto takes lots of pictures of places, plants and animals that are new to him. He also tastes different types of local food, and a variety of new fruits and vegetables.

Enrique spends much of his time studying the traditions and legends of *La India Dormida*. He talks to various people in the area, takes notes in his notebook and writes down his plans to help the local community.

Two weeks have passed, and the boys are going back to Spain in a few days. It is time to prepare for their airplane trip.

---

8 spend more time – pasar (más) tiempo

18 — See You Soon!

The day arrives to return to Spain. Lily drives Enrique to the airport while they enjoy a long conversation in the car. Next, Beto arrives with his host family. Beto says goodbye to his family and walks towards Enrique and Lily; they stop for a moment, greet each other and talk a little more. Beto is as always a little nervous about boarding the airplane...

—"Well Lily, we have to say goodbye!" Enrique says in a sad voice.

—"I will see you soon, Enrique!" Lily says. "Remember that next summer I'm going to Spain."

—"Yes, guys, it's okay! We will see each other soon!" Beto says nervously. "Now, at this moment, I'm worried about traveling by airplane again!"

Enrique says, "Beto, this is the last part of our adventure in Panama. Everything is going to be okay!"

The three of them give each other a big hug and say goodbye. They know they will be together again in Spain next summer.

Enrique and Lily look at each other in the eyes and smile. Enrique's face doesn´t turn red like a tomato, but he feels a little nervous. They share their contact information on social media and promise to keep in touch. Lily is very enthusiastic to go to Spain.

—"Once again Lily, thanks to you and your parents for being so kind with me," Enrique says. "I really enjoyed Panama and want to come back and visit in the future again. I love everything about Panama."

—"I loved everything too, especially the food! I'm hungry again! Ha ha! Well, see you soon Lily," Beto says.

Happy, Enrique and Beto enter the giant airplane that is going to take them to Spain.

19 — Back to Spain with a Sustainable Plan

After a long trip, the boys arrive in Spain. At the airport, they hug, say goodbye, and go home with their parents.

At Enrique's house, his mother prepares a delicious dinner. They all sit down to eat and talk about the trip. Enrique's father looks at him and says:

—"Enrique, tell us more about your adventure in Panama."

Enrique tells them the details about *El Valle*, *La India Dormida* Mountain, their hiking trip, its history, the Sunday market and the experience at *La Posada de Rosa Inn*. He also tells them about Lily, her family and the vision of *Flor del Aire* that he saw on mountain.

—"Mom and Dad! You're going to think I'm crazy, but the most interesting part of this trip was literally the vision! A VISION!"

—"What are you saying, Enrique?" the mother asks.

—"When Beto and I walked along the trail, we saw a vision of the spirit of *La India Dormida* of the mountain. Right there at that moment, I knew about the main reason why I visited Panama," Enrique continues speaking with enthusiasm. "Now I have a great idea for my graduation project. It is about agriculture and natural resources because I already know what I want to study at the university! I want to be an agronomist engineer!"

—"Excellent!" comments the father. We really like that you came back from your trip so enthusiastic, so your trip was everything you wanted it to be and more. Now tell us more about your idea for the project, **we are all ears**[1].

Enrique explains his idea to help SSID with the reforestation of the mountain.

—"The idea is that for my graduation Capstone project I am going to make an ecological **proposal**[2] for *El Valle* and *La India Dormida* Mountain, but I am going to need your help. I want to be part of the *Sociedad Secreta de La India Dormida* (SSID) to work in the preservation of the mountain."

—"Enrique, that's a great idea!" his father assures.

—"How do you plan to do it?" the mother asks.

Enrique continues talking "First, with Lily's help I am going to join the Society (SSID) as a member. My idea is to organize the community to reforest *La India Dormida* Mountain with Panamanian sunflowers. Panamanian sunflowers are not an invasive species. Second, with the Society I will organize the **harvesting**[3] of the sunflowers to sell, or to extract oil and seeds. They can also sell the flowers and products at the Sunday open-market."

---

1 we are all ears - somos todo oído.
2 proposal – propuesta con una idea de proyecto.
3 harvesting - cosecha

The father says, "Wonderful idea Enrique, in time this project will help the people of the town because it can be a strong industry for the future of the community."

The mother exclaims, "I think your idea is great. You need to present the project to your teacher soon."

Then the father shares some very important historical and family information.

—"You know Enrique, the original sunflower seeds that started our business came from Latin America. Our ancestor Carlos Dominguez met an Indigenous girl on one of his exploration trips. She showed him the fields of sunflowers, and he brought the seed back to Spain as a transplant gift. I believe the girl was from Panama."

—"What a coincidence!" Enrique smiles and exclaims.

—"Destiny is really crazy, isn't it? Destiny took you to Panama to find out a little more about sunflowers, wow!" the father assures.

—"Enrique we are proud of you because you are interested in learning about your family's history. Also, your encouragement to reforest the land is a great idea. We want to support you in your idea for the project," the mother says.

—"Yes! Double Wow! Now it all makes more sense!" Enrique says with a happy face. "Especially because reforestation helps the mountain, the Indigenous people, and the people of the village. Mom and Dad, you are examples of **kindness**[4]. I am very proud of our family."

---

4 kindness - bondad

Enrique and his parents smile and continue eating. At the end of dinner, Enrique looks at his cellular phone and says:

"I am going to contact Lily and SSID to start with the ecological proposal. First, I'm going to start on social media with the #Panama #girasolestiktok #indiadormida. Also, when Lily visits us next summer, you guys will meet her. I know you will love her; she is a pretty, nice, and intelligent girl, ha!"

The end?

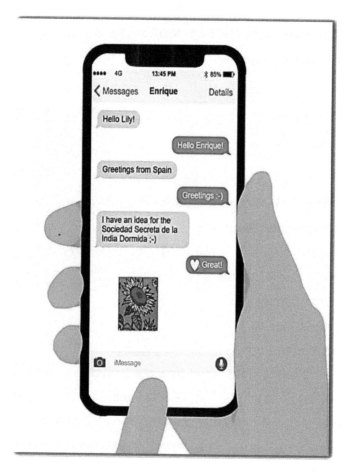

Glossary

A

A/an - un(a)/uno(s)

able - poder

about - acerca de

above - encima

accept - aceptar

acquaintance - conocido

actions - acciones,

activities - actividades

adds - agrega

admire - admirar

admires - él/ella admira

adults - adultos

adventure(s) - aventura(s)adventurous – aventurero

aerial - aéreo

afraid - asustado

after(that)-después(de eso)

afternoon - tarde

again - de nuevo

against - en contra

age - edad

agricultura - agricultura

agronomist - agrónomo

ahead - adelante

air - aire

airplane - avión

airport - aeropuerto

alarm - alarma

alike - similar

all - todo/ todos

allow/allowed - permitir/permitido

almost - casi

alone - solo

along - a lo largo de

alongside - junto a

already – ya

also - además

although - a pesar de que

always - siempre

amazed - asombrado

amazement - asombro

amazing - increíble

America - América

American - americano

among - entre

ancestor(s) - ancestro(s) /antepasado(s)

and – y

animals - animales

answer(s) - respuesta(s)

any - ninguna

anything - cualquier cosa

appears - aparece

appreciate(s) - aprecio

appreciative - agradecido

approaches - se acerca/se aproxima

April - abril

are - ellos(as) son

área - zona/área

around - alrededor

arrival - llegada

arrive(d) - llegar/llegaron

arrives - él/ella llega

as – como

ask(s) preguntar, él/ella pregunta

asleep - dormido

assures - asegura

at - a

ate – él/ella comió

athletic - atlético

Atlantic - Atlántico

atended - asistió

attention - atención

attentive - atento

attract - atraer

audio - audio

August - agosto

avenida- avenida

avoid - evitar

away - fuera

awesome - increíble

B

Back - espalda

Backpacks - mochilas

balboa, Panamanian currency - balboa, moneda panameña

bank - banco

banking - bancario

bars - barras

battery(ies) - batería(s)

bay - bahía

be - ser

beach(es) - playa(s)

beats - late

beautiful -hermosa

0

because -porque

before - antes de

begins - él/ella comienza

being - ser

believe - creer

bell - campana

belong - pertenecer

besides - además

best/better - mejor

between - entre

BFF - mejor amigo(a)

big - grande

birds - aves

birthday - cumpleaños

black - negro

blanket - manta

blue - azul

boarding - embarque, abordaje

boat - bote

body - cuerpo

boots- botas

bored/boring - aburrido/aburrido

boss - jefe

both - ambos

bottles - botellas

boy(s) - niño(s)

brave - valiente

breakfast - desayuno

bridge - puente

bring - traer

brochure - folleto

broken - roto

brought - trajo

building - edificio

business - negocio

busy - ocupado

but - pero

buy - comprar

by- por

Bye!- ¡Adiós!

C

Cacique – indigenous chief

call(s)/called - llamar /él,ella llama /llamado

calls - llamadas

calm - calma

came - llegó

can/cannot - poder/no poder

canal - canal

candies - dulces

Capstone Project - Proyecto final

car(s) - carro/coche(s)

care - cuidado

carefully - con cuidado

carimañolas - frituras hechas de puré de yuca

Casco Viejo - Ciudad colonial en Panamá

Catholic - católico

causes - causas

center - centrar

central - central

ceramic - cerámico

cereal - cereal

Cerro Ancón hill - Cerro Ancón

challenge - desafío, reto

chance - el chance/ la oportunidad

change - cambiar

chaperones – chaperones /acompañantes

cheaper - más económico/barato

check - cheque

cheek(s) - la(s) mejilla(s)

cheerful - alegre

cheese - queso

chest - pecho

chicheme - una bebida de Panamá hecha de maíz dulce

chicken - pollo

chief – jefe(a)

children - niños

chuckle – risa baja y entre dientes

Cinta Costera - Coastal Beltway

city(ies) - ciudad(s)

claim - afirmar

class(es) - clase(s)

climate - clima

climatic - climático

climb - escalada

clock - reloj

close - cerrar

closer - más cerca

clothes - ropa

coasts - costas

coconut - coco

code - código

coffee - café

coin – moneda

coincidence -coincidencia

cold - frío

college - universidad

colonial - de los tiempos coloniales

colonization -colonización

colors - colores

combing - peinando

come up - sube

comfortable - cómodo

coming - viniendo

comment(s)- comentario(s)

common - común

communicate -comunicar

community - comunidad

complete -completo

confirms - confirma

confused - confundido

connection - conexión

connects - conecta

construction - construcción

contact/ed - contacto /contactado

continent - continente

continue(s) - seguir, continúa

conversation - conversacion

cooks - cocineros

cool off - refrescarse

cool! - ¡Genial!

cooler - más frío

coordinate - coordinar

copper - cobre, mineral

cordillera - cordillera, cadena montañosa - Corredor Sur autopista del sur

costa - costa

costera - costera

country(ies) - país(es)

countryside - campo, interior

couple - pareja

courage - coraje,valentía

courageous - valiente

course - curso

covered - cubierto

cráter - cráter

crazy - loco

create - crear

Crocs - Calzado de la marca Crocs

crowd - multitud

crowing – cacareo

crying - llanto

cultivate - cultivar

culture/cultural - cultura/cultural

curious - curioso

currency, money - moneda, dinero

cut - recorte

D

dad - padre

daily - a diario

damage - daño

damaged -estropeado

dance - danza

danger - peligro

dark - oscuro

data - datos

daughter - hija

day off - día libre

day(s) - dias)

dead - muerto

December - diciembre

declines – él/ella declina

delicious - delicioso

descendant(s)- descendientes)

describes - describe

design - diseño

despair - desesperación

dessert - postre

destiny - destino

detail(s)- detalle(s)

died - fallecido

difference - diferencia

different - diferente

dining - comida

dinner - cena

dip - aderezo

disappears – él/ella desaparece

distance - distancia

distributes – él/ella distribuye

do/did - hacer/hizo

does/doesn't - hace/no hace

doing - haciendo

dollar - dólar

dominoes - dominó

don't//didn't - no // no

done - hecho

door - puerta

dormant – latente

double - doble

dough - masa

down - abajo

dream - sueño

drinks - bebidas

drinks - él/ella bebe

drive - conducir

driver - conductor

drives - conduce

driving - conduciendo

drops - gotas

dry - seco

dry off - secar

Duke - Duque

Dulce Tres Leches
(dessert) - Dulce Tres
Leches (postre)

during - durante

E

each - cada

eagerly - con entusiasmo

early - temprano

earn - ganar

ears - orejas

earth - tierra

easy - fácil

eat/eats, eating - comer/
él/ella come, comiendo

ecological - ecológico

economy - economía

ecosystem - ecosistema

edge - borde

eight - ocho

either - cualquiera

elves - elfos

embarrassed -
avergonzado

empanada(s) -
empanadas son discos de
masa rellenos y cocidos
fritos u horneados.

enchanted - encantada

encouragement - ánimo

end - fin

energy - energía

engaged - comprometido

engineer - ingeniero

engineering - ingeniería

English - inglés

enjoy(ed) -
disfrutar/disfruté

enjoys - él/ella disfruta

enough - suficiente

enter - ingresar

entering - entrando

enthusiasm - entusiasmo

enthusiastic - entusiasta

entrance - entrada

entrepreneurship -
emprendimiento

eruption - erupción

especially -especialmente

established - establecido

eternal - eterno

Europe - Europa

European - europeo

euros – moneda europea

even - incluso

every/everyone -
todos/todos

everything - todo

everywhere - en todas
partes

examples - ejemplos

excellent - excelente

exchange - intercambio

excited/excitedly -
emocionado

excitement - emoción

excites - emociona, anima

exclaims - exclama

exists - existe

exit - salida

experience(s) -
experiencia(s)

experts - expertos

explains - explica

explanation - explicación

exploration - exploración

explore - explorar

explorer(s) -
explorador(es)

extract - extraer

eyes - ojos

F

face - rostro

falls out – caerse

familiar - familiar,
conocido(a)

family(ies) - familia(s)

famous - famoso

fantastic - fantástico

farm - granja

fascinating - fascinante

fast - rápido

father - padre

favorite - favorito

feel(s) - él/ella siente,
ellos/ellas sienten

feeling - sentimiento

feet - pies

fell asleep - se quedó
dormida

felt - él/ella sintió

few - pocos

field(s) - los campos)

finally - por fin

find - encontrar

finds - él/ella encuentra

fine - multa

finish(es) – terminar, él/ella termina

first - primero

five - cinco

flag - bandera

flavors - sabores

flies - moscas

flight(s) - vuelo(s)

flip flops - chancletas, chanclas

flower(s) - flor(s)

flyer - volantes

flying - volador

follow - seguir

food - comida

for - por

forest - bosque

forever - para siempre

forget - olvidar

forms - eso forma

fought - luchó

found - encontró

found out - averiguado

four - cuatro

fragrance - fragancia

fresh – nuevo

friend(s) - amigo(s)

friendlier - más amigable

frightened - aterrado

frog(s) - rana(s)

from - desde

fruits - frutas

full - completo, lleno

fun/funny - divertido/a

further - más lejos

future - futuro

G

game(s) - juego(s)

garbage - basura

gate - portón

gather - recolectar

get(s)/got – ob/tener// él/ella ob/tiene, ob/tuvo

gets very red – se sonroja

gets up - se levanta

ghost(s) - fantasma(s)

giant - gigante

gift – regalo

girl(s) – niña(s), chica(s), muchacha(s)

give(s) – dar, él/ella da

glad - contento

go/goes-ir/voy/va/vamos

goal - meta

goblins - duendes

god(s) – Dios(es)

going - yendo

gold - oro

golden - dorado

good - bien

goodbye – adios

goodness - bondad

government - gobierno

GPS - (por sus siglas en inglés) Sistema de Posicionamiento Global

Grade grado - escolar

graduate (will) - graduan/graduarán

graduation - graduación

grandfather - abuelo

grass - hierba, grama, pasto

great - genial

greatly - muy

green - verde

greet(s) - saludar/saluda

ground - suelo

groups - grupos

guardian - guardián(a)

guests - huéspedes

guides - guías

guys - los chicos(as)

ha ha! onomatopoeia for laughing ja ja! - onomatopeya para reír

had - tener/tenía

hair - cabello

half - medio

hand(s) - mano(s)

handicrafts - artesanias, manualidades

handsome - guapo

happened, happening- sucedió, sucediendo

happily, happy - felizmente, feliz, contento

hard - duro

harm - dañar

harvesting - cosecha

hat(s) - sombreros

hate - odio

have, has – tener, él/ella tiene

having - teniendo

he, him, his - él (pronombre), él (objeto de pron.), su (posesivo)

head - cabeza

hear - oír

heart - corazón

heart beating –latiendo (corazón)

Hello! Hi! - ¡Hola! ¡Hola!

help, helped, helping - ayudar, ayudar, ayudar

helps - él/ella ayuda

hens - gallinas

here - aquí

Hey! - ¡Oye!

Hieroglyphics - jeroglíficos

high, highest - alto, más alto

highway - autopista

hiking - senderismo

hill(s) - colina, sierras

historical - histórico

history - historia

home - casa

hope, hopes, I hope that - esperar

Ojalá(que) - esperar que

horses - caballos

hospitable - hospitalario

host(ess) - anfitrión(a)

hot - caliente

hotel - hotel

hour(s) - hora(s)

house - casa

how - como, cómo

hug(s) - abrazo(s)

huge - enorme

humid - húmedo

hundred, one hundred - centenas, cien

hungry - hambriento

hurry - apurarse

I

I - yo

I am - Yo soy/ yo estoy

I am eager to... - Tengo ganas de...

I have - yo tengo

I have been here for only... - Solo he estado aquí ...

I imagine - yo imagino

I will - voy a

I will/I´ll - Yo haré

Idea - idea

immediate, immediately - inmediato, de inmediato

immerse yourself – sumergirte

immortalized- inmortalizado

important – importante

impressed- impresionado

improve - mejorar

in, into - en, en

India Dormida - Nombre propio de la montaña en Panamá.

India – indigenous, india, amerindia, indígena

industry - industria

information -información

inn - posada, hostal

innovation - innovación

instead - en lugar de

intelligent - inteligente

interest, interested - interés, interesado

interesting - interesante

international- internacional

Internet - Internet

introduce - introducir

invasive invasor

invitation - invitación

is - él/ella es

isn't - él/ella no es

isthmus – istmo es una estrecha franja de tierra que une dos más grandes.

it - eso

It looks cool! - ¡Se ve genial!

it's, its - es, su

J

join - unirse

journey - viaje

joy - alegría

juice – jugo

jumped él/ella saltó

jumps él/ella salta

just - solo

K

keep - guardar

key - clave

kids - niños

kilometers - kilómetros

kind, kindness - amable, amabilidad

king - rey

kiss(es) - beso(s)

kitchen - cocina

know, he/she knows, knew - saber, él / ella sabe, supo

known - conocido

L

lady - dama

land - tierra

landowner - terrateniente

lands - tierras

landscapes - paisajes

large - grande

last - último

late - tarde

later - luego

laugh - reír

laughing - risa

laughs - él/ella se ríe

lava - lava (volcán)

leader - líder

learn, learns - él/ella aprende, ellos/ellas aprende

learned - él/ella aprendió

learning - aprendiendo

leave - abandonar

left - izquierda, solo quedan

legend(s) - leyenda(s)

less - menos

lesson - lección

let - dejar

let's - vamos

level - nivel

life - la vida

like (verb) /like (similar) - gustar (verbo) / parecerse (similar)

likes - a él/ella le gusta

listen, listens, listened - escucha, él/ella escucha, escuchado

listening - escuchando

listens - escucha

literally - literalmente

littering - tirar basura

little - pequeño, poco

live, lives - vivir, él/ella vive

living - viviendo

local - local

local people, locals - gente local, lugareños

located - situado

location - localización

logo - logo

lonely - solitario

long - largo

look(s) like - parece

looking - buscando

looks - él/ella mira

lost - perdió

lot(s) - lote(s)

love, loves, loved - amor, él/ella ama, amado

lover - amante

loyalty - lealtad

luck, lucky - suerte, afortunado

lunch - comida

M

macaws - guacamayos, guacamayas

made - hecho

magic - magia

main - principal

mainland - continente

maintain - mantener

make, makes - hacer, él/ella hace

man - hombre

mango (oes) - mango(s)

many - muchos

many years ago - hace muchos años

map(s) - mapa(s)

March - Marzo

market - mercado

married - casado

mathematics - matemáticas

maybe - quizás

me, tell me - me (objeto de pronombre), dime

meaning - significado, sentido

means - eso significa

meat - carne

media - medios de comunicación

meet(s) - reunir, conocer, él/ella conoce

member(s) - miembro(s)

mention - mencionar

met - reunió

meters - metros

metro - metro, modo de transportación

middle - medio

mild - suave, ligero

miles - millas

milk - leche

minutes - minutos

miss - extranar

mission - misión

mobile(s) - móvil(es)

modern - moderno

mom - mamá

moment - momento

money - dinero

monkeys - monos

monte - monte, montaña

monument – monumento

more - más

morning - mañana

most - la mayoría

mother(s) - madre(s)

mountain(s) - montañas)

move, moving - moverse, moviendo

moza - término formal y antiguo para una joven doncella

Mr., Mrs., Miss - Señor, señora, señorita

much - mucho

museum - museo

my - mi

myself - yo mismo

myths - mitos

N

name(s) - nombre(s)

named - llamado

nap - siesta

narrow - angosta

national - nacional

native - nativo

natural, nature - natural, naturaleza

navel - ombligo

near - cerca

need, needs - necesitar, él/ella necesita, necesidad

nervous - nervioso

nervously - nerviosamente

never - nunca

new - nuevo

next - próximo

nice - bonito

nice people - gente amable

nickname - apodo

night - noche

no, not - no, no

noble - noble, aristócrata (m & f)

nobody - nadie

noise - ruido

nor - ni

normal - normal

north - norte

notebook - cuaderno, libreta

notes - notas

notice(s) - aviso(s)

November - noviembre

now - ahora

number - número

numerous - numeroso

O

observes - él/ella observa

obvious - obvio

ocean(s) - océano(s)

of - de

offering - ofrecimiento

offers, offered - él/ella ofrece, ofreció

Oh - Oh

oil - aceite

okay - okey

old, oldest - viejo, más viejo o antiguo

on - en

once - una vez

one - uno

only - solamente

open-market - mercado abierto

opens - él/ella abre

opportunity - oportunidad

or - o

orange - naranja

orchid(s) - orquídea(s)

organize - organizar

origin, original - origen, original

other/another - otro/otra

our - nuestro(a)

out - afuera

outdoor - exterior

over - sobre

overwhelmed - abrumado

own - propio

owners - propietarios

P

Pacific - Pacífico

pack - paquete

Panama La Vieja - La ciudad antigua de Panamá

panamanian - panameño

panic - pánico

paper - papel

paradise - paraíso

parents - padres

park - parque

parking - estacionamiento

parque - parque

part - parte

passed - aprobado

password - clave, palabra secreta

path - sendero, camino

patio - patio

peace - paz

peaceful - tranquilo

penny(ies) - centavo(s)

people - gente

pepper - pimienta

perfect - perfecto

permit - permiso

person - persona

petroglyphs - petroglifos

Phew! - ¡Uf!

phone(s), cellular phone, cellphone - teléfono(s), teléfono celular, teléfono celular

pick up - recoger

picked up - recogido

picture(s) - foto(s)

piece - trozo

Piedra Pintada - Piedra Pintada o painted stone

pig - cerdo

place(s) - lugare(s)

plan(s) - plan(s)

plants - plantas

plátanos maduros - plátanos maduros

play soccer - jugar fútbol

play video games - jugar video juegos

played - jugó

playing - jugando

plaza - plaza

pleasant - agradable

please - por favor

plenty - mucho

plus - más

pocket - bolsillo

podcast - pódcast

points - puntos

popular - popular

pork - cerdo

posada - posada

possibility - posibilidad

potato - patata, papa

practice - práctica

precious - precioso

prepare, prepares - preparar, él/ella prepara

present - regalo, presente

preservation - preservación

pretty - bonita

previous - anterior

princess - princesa

probably - probablemente

problem(s) - problemas)

products - productos

program - programa

project(s) - proyecto(s)

promise, promised - promesa, prometida

properly – apropiadamente, adecuadamente

proposal - propuesta

proud - orgulloso

provides - proporciona

puente - puente

punctual - puntual

purse - bolso

put(s) - poner, él/ella pone

Q

Queen - Reina

question - pregunta

¡Quiquiriquí! - Onomatopeya para el sonido de un gallo.

quick, quickly - rápido rápidamente

quietly - en silencio

R

races - razas

rains, rainy, raining - lluvias, lluvioso, lloviendo

rating - clasificación

rays - rayos

reach - alcanzar

reaction - reacción

read, reads - lee, él/ella lee

ready - Listo

real, reality, really - real, realidad, de verdad

realizing - dándose cuenta

reason - razón

receives, received - él/ella recibe, recibió

recommendation - recomendación

recommends - él/ella recomienda

red - rojo

reforest, reforestation - repoblación forestal, reforestar

refreshing - refrescante

region - región

relieved - aliviado

remain - permanecer, mantener

remained - se mantuvo

remember(s) - recuerda, le recuerda

reminds him, reminds them - le recuerda, les recuerda

RENFE - The National Network of Spanish Railways, it has High Speed (AVE) trains. - RENFE – abreviatura para Red Nacional de Ferrocarriles Españoles, cuenta con trenes de Alta Velocidad (AVE)

resisted – resistido, él/ella resitió

resources - recursos

respect - respeto

respectful - respetuoso

respecting - respecto a

respond, responds - responde, él/ella responde

rest - descanso

result - resultado

return - regresar

rice - arroz

ride - montar

right - derecho

ring(s) - anillo(s)

rises - sube

river - río

road - la carretera

rock(s) - roca(s)

romantic, romanticism - romantico, romanticismo

room - habitación

roosters - gallos

rumors - rumores

run errands - hacer recados, diligencias

s

sad, sadly - triste, tristemente

said - dijeron

salad - ensalada

salt - sal

salto - salto

same - mismo

sappy - cursi

Saturday - sábado

saw - vi, viste, vio, vimos, vieron

say, says, saying - decir, él/ella dice, diciendo

scan - escanear

scared - asustado

scary - de miedo

scent - olor

school(s) - escuela(s)

science - ciencia

screams - gritos y carcajadas

screen - pantalla

sea(s) - mar (es)

search - búsqueda

season(s) - temporada(s), estación(es)

second(s) - segundos)

secret - secreto

secreta - secreta

section - sección

seed(s) - semilla(s)

seem - parecer

sees - él/ella ve

selfie - foto selfi

sell, sells, selling - vender, él/ella vende, vendiendo

sensational - sensacional

sense - sentido

separated - apartado

seriously - seriamente

set - colocar

seven - siete

several - varios

shakes - sacudidas, temblores

shall - deberá

shape, shaped - forma, con forma de

share, shares - compartir, él/ella comparte

she, her, hers - ella (pronombre), ella (objeto de pron.), su (posesivo)

she's - ella es

shiny - brillante

shoes - zapatos

short - corto, pequeño

should - debería

shout, shouts - gritar, él/ella grita

showed - él/ella presentó

shut up - cállate

side - lado

sign - letrero

signal - señal

silhouette - silueta

silly - tonto

since - ya que

sing - canta

sit, sits - sentarse, se sienta

skyscrapers - rascacielos

sleep, sleeping - dormir, durmiendo, dormido(a)

slopes - pendientes, falda, ladera

sloth bear - oso perezoso

slowly - despacio

small, smaller - pequeño, más pequeño

smart - inteligente

smartphone(s) - teléfono(s) inteligente(s)

smile(s) - sonrisa(s)

snack(s) - merienda(s)

snakes - serpientes, culebras

sneakers - zapatillas, zapatos deportivos, tenis

so - asi que

soaked - mojado

soccer - fútbol

social - social

society - sociedad

solutions - soluciones

some - algunos

someday - algún día

soon - pronto

sorry - lo siento

Sounds exciting! - ¡Suena emocionante!

Sounds perfect - Suena perfecto

south - Sur

souvenirs - souvenirs

Spain - España

Spaniard - español, la ciudadanía

Spanish - Español, el idioma

sparkle - brillar

speak, speaks, speaking - hablar, él/ella habla, hablando

special - especial

species - especies

spend (more) time – pasar (más) tiempo

spiders - arañas

spirit(s) - espíritu)

spring(s) - nacimientos de aguas

square - cuadrado

star - estrella

start, started - empezar, empezo

stay, stays, staying - quedarse, él/ella quedarse, quedando

steep - empinado

steps - pasos

stew - estofado

sticker - pegatina

still - todavía

stone - roca

stop, stopping - parar, detener, parando

store - tienda

story - historia

strange, strangest - extraño, mas extraño

strategic - estratégico

strong, stronger - fuerte, más fuerte

student(s) - estudiantes)

study, studying - estudiar, estudiando

stuffed - relleno (a)

such - tal

suddenly - de repente, repentinamente

suffered - sufrió

suitcases - maletas

summer - verano

sun - sol

Sunday(s) - domingo(s)

sunflower(s) - girasol(s)

sunglasses - gafas de sol

sunlight - luz de sol

super - súper

support- apoyo

surprise, surprised - sorpresa, sorprendido

sustainable - sostenible

sweaty - sudoroso

sweet - dulce

swim, swims - nadar, él/ella nada

swimming - natación

symbol - símbolo

system - sistema

T

table - mesa

take, taking - tomar, tomando

taken - tomado

takes - él/ella toma, lleva

takes a shower - ducha

takes out - saca

tales - cuentos

talk, talks, talking - hablar, él/ella habla, hablando

talked (I, she) - hablé, habló

tall- alto

tapir or wild pig - tapir o jabalí - macho de monte

tastes - sabores

teacher(s) - maestro(a)(s)

tell, tells - decir, él/ella dice

temperatura(s) – temperatura(s)

temporary -temporal

ten - diez

tents - carpas

text(s) - texto(s)

texting - mensajes de texto

tan - que

thank, thanks - gracias

that, those - que, aquellos

the - la

their - sus

them, themselves - ellos, ellos mismos

then - luego

there are - existen

there is, there are - hay, hay

thermal - térmico

they - ellos

thing(s) - cosa(s)

think, thinks - pensar, él/ella piensa

thirty - treinta

this, these - este, estos

those - esos

though - sin embargo

thought - pensamiento

three - tres

throat - garganta

through - mediante

Tik Tok - Tik Tok red social

time - tiempo

time off - tiempo libre

tired - cansado

title - título

to - para

today - hoy

together - juntos

told - dijo

tomato - tomate

tomorrow - mañana

tonight - esta noche

too - también

took - tomó

top - cima

top it off - por si fuera poco

topic - tema

toucans - tucanes

touch, touches, touched - tocar, él/ella toca, tocó

tour - gira

tourism - turismo

tourist(s) - turista(s)

towards - hacia

town - ciudad, pueblo

townspeople - gente del pueblo

traditions - tradiciones

traffic - tráfico

trails - caminos

train - tren

transplant - trasplante

travel, traveled - yo viajo, viajé //él/ella viaja, viajó

travelers - viajeros

traveling - viajando

tres - árboles

tremor(s) - temblor(es)

tres - tres

tribe(s) - tribu(s)

tries - él/ella trata

trip(s) - viaje(s), excursione(s)

tropical - tropical

truth - verdad

turn, turns - girar, él/ella gira

two - dos

types - tipos

typical - típico

U

Uber - Transportation company with an app

Uff! - ¡Uff! sonido de alivio

unable - incapaz

under - bajo

understand, understands - entender, él/ella entiende

universo - universo

university - Universidad

until - hasta

unusual - raro

up - arriba

use, uses, used - uso, él/ella usa, usado

usually - generalmente

V

Valley - valle

variety - variedad

various - varios

vegetables - verduras

vegetation - vegetación

very - muy

video - video

view - vista

village - pueblo

vinegar - vinagre

visible - visible

visión - visión

visit, visits - visitar, él/ella visita

visited(I) - visité(yo)

visitors - visitantes

voice(s) - voz(s)

volcano - volcán

W

waist - cintura

waiting- esperando

wakes, waking - despierta, despertando

walk, walks, walking - caminar, él/ella camina, caminando

walked (I) - caminé

walks up (he) - camina hacia (él)

wandering - vagando

want, wants, you wanted- querer, él/ella quiere, quisiste

warrior - guerrero

was - fue

watch - ver

water(s) - agua(s)

waterfall(s) - cascada(s)

waterproof - impermeable

waterway - canal navegable

waves - saluda (con las manos)

way - via

we, us - nosotros

wear, wearing - llevar, llevando

weather - tiempo

website - sitio web

week(s), weekend(s) - semana(s), fin (es) de semana(s)

welcome - bienvenidos

well - bien

what - qué

when - cuándo

where - donde, dónde

which - cuales, cuáles

while - mientras

White - blanco

who - quien, quién

whose - de quien, cuyo

why - por qué

wild - salvaje

will - voluntad

wind, windy - viento, ventoso

with, without - con, sin

woman, women - mujer, mujeres

won't - no lo haré

wonder - preguntarse

wonderful - maravilloso

wonders - maravillas

wood - madera

Wooohooo!- ¡Wooohooo!

work, works, working - trabajar, él/ella trabaja, trabajando

world - mundo

worry, worried - preocuparse, preocupado

worth - valor

would - haría

Wow! - ¡Guau!

Writes - él/ella escribe

wrong - equivocado

Y

Yay!- Hurra!

year - año

yellow - amarillo

yes - sí

you - tú

you're - estás

young - joven

your, yours - tus tuyo

yucca - yuca

yummy - delicioso

Z

zoo – zoológico

About the Author

Nayka Barrios Jaén, also known as Señora Miller, is a Panamanian-American author. She is also a Spanish instructor. Nayka graduated from the *Instituto Nacional de Panamá*, she has a Business Degree from the *Universidad del Istmo, Panamá;* has a Master's Degree in Applied Linguistics from the *Universidad de Jaén, Andalucía, España*. She also holds a Postgraduate Certificate in Higher Education from Harvard University, USA.

Nayka was born in *Panamá* and used to spend summers with her *abuela Frede* in *Bejuco* which is a village near *El Valle* and *La India Dormida* Mountain, where the legend and the story take place. Nayka is passionate about her native *Panamá*, and the Spanish language preservation. As an educator she is also enthusiastic about teaching young generations to respect other cultures and to protect the environment through sustainable initiatives.